Mar 18

Does
VOTING
Matter?

By Leslie Beckett

KidHaven
PUBLISHING

Published in 2018 by
KidHaven Publishing, an Imprint of Greenhaven Publishing, LLC
353 3rd Avenue
Suite 255
New York, NY 10010

Designer: Seth Hughes
Editor: Katie Kawa

Photo credits: Cover © iStockphoto.com/fstop123; p. 5 (top and bottom) Blend Images - Hill Street Studios/Brand X Pictures/Getty Images; p. 7 DNetromphotos/Shutterstock.com; p. 9 (left) Drew Angerer/Getty Images; p. 9 (right) Scott Olson/Getty Images; p. 11 Hero Images/Getty Images; p. 13 © iStockphoto.com/Teamjackson; p. 15 (top) Herbert Gehr/The LIFE Images Collection/Getty Images; p. 15 (bottom) Paul Thompson/Topical Press Agency/Getty Images; p. 17 Camrocker/iStock/Thinkstock; p. 19 Jeff Swensen/Getty Images; p. 21 (notepad) ESB Professional/Shutterstock.com; p. 21 (markers) Kucher Serhii/Shutterstock.com; p. 21 (photo frame) FARBAI/iStock/Thinkstock; p. 21 (inset, left) LOGAN CYRUS/AFP/Getty Images; p. 21 (inset, middle-left) bizoo_n/iStock/Thinkstock; p. 21 (inset, middle-right) IcemanJ/iStock/Thinkstock; p. 21 (inset, right) Ron Jenkins/Getty Images.

Library of Congress Cataloging-in-Publication Data

Names: Beckett, Leslie, author.
Title: Does voting matter? / Leslie Beckett.
Description: New York : KidHaven Publishing, 2018. | Series: Points of view |
  Includes index.
Identifiers: LCCN 2017051337| ISBN 9781534524927 (6 pack) | ISBN
  9781534524293 (library bound book) | ISBN 9781534524910 (pbk. book)
Subjects: LCSH: Voting–United States–Juvenile literature. |
  Elections–United States–Juvenile literature. | Political
  participation–United States–Juvenile literature. | Democracy–United
  States–Juvenile literature.
Classification: LCC JK1978 .B435 2018 | DDC 323.60973–dc23
LC record available at https://lccn.loc.gov/2017051337

Printed in the United States of America

CPSIA compliance information: Batch #CW18KL: For further information contact Greenhaven Publishing LLC, New York, New York at 1-844-317-7404.

Please visit our website, www.greenhavenpublishing.com. For a free color catalog of all our high-quality books, call toll free 1-844-317-7404 or fax 1-844-317-7405.

CONTENTS

VOTING

Voting is an important part of life in a democratic country such as the United States. Elections are held for many local and national government positions—from city council members and mayors to governors and the president. Voting in these elections allows citizens to have a say in choosing their leaders.

Although voting is at the center of the democratic **process**, many people don't vote. They believe their vote doesn't matter. Why do some people have this point of view? Read on to learn more about the different views on voting!

Know the Facts!

In the United States, people 18 years old and older can register, or formally sign up, to vote.

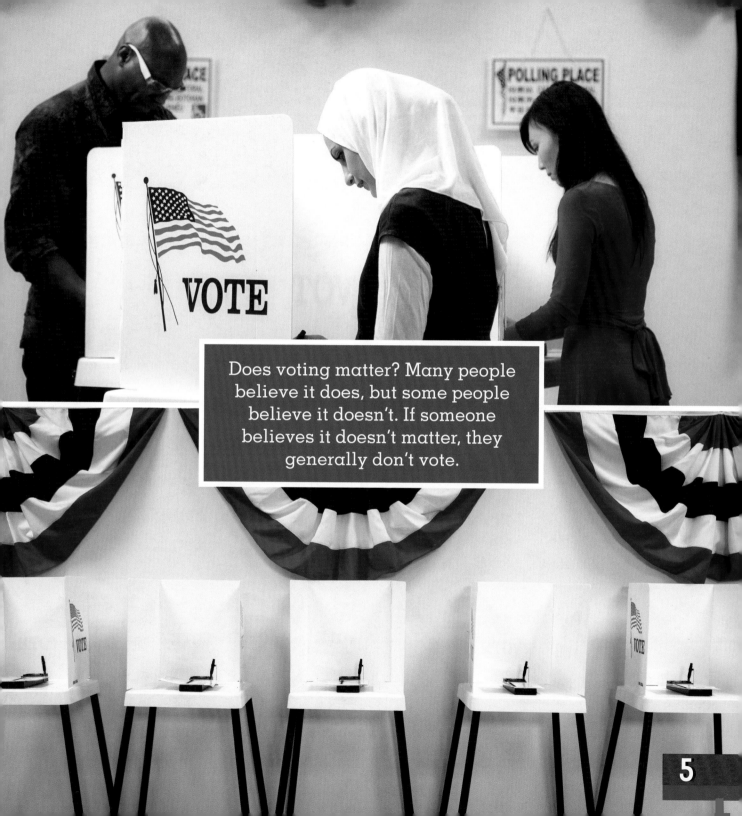

Does voting matter? Many people believe it does, but some people believe it doesn't. If someone believes it doesn't matter, they generally don't vote.

Electing ELECTORS

Many **debates** about the importance of voting are centered on the Electoral College. This is a system set up in the U.S. Constitution for electing the president. When a citizen votes for a presidential **candidate**, they're actually voting for that candidate's group of electors. The electors then vote for the president.

The Electoral College exists to give states with smaller populations a more equal voice in the election of a president. It also exists because some of the Founding Fathers didn't believe common citizens should choose such an important leader.

Know the Facts!

As of 2017, the Electoral College has 538 members, and 270 electoral votes are needed for someone to be elected president.

How the United States Voted in 2016

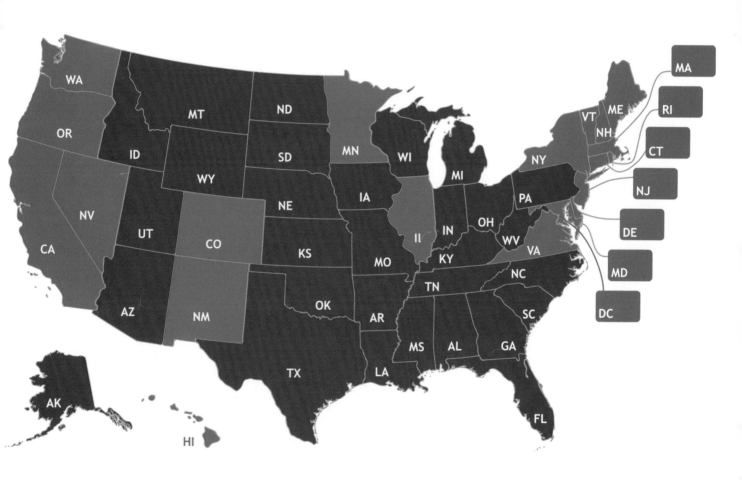

| Democrat | Republican |

The majority of the electoral votes from the red states on this map went to Donald Trump in 2016. The blue states' electoral votes went mainly to Hillary Clinton.

ELECTORAL VOTE

The Electoral College system can sometimes make people feel as if their vote doesn't matter. Because of the way the Electoral College is set up, there have been times in U.S. history when the winner of the **popular vote** didn't win the electoral vote and, as such, didn't become president. This happened in the 1824, 1876, 1888, 2000, and 2016 presidential elections.

When this happens, the election results don't match up with what the majority of voters wanted. This can make those voters feel as if their voice wasn't heard.

Know the Facts!

In the 2016 presidential election, Hillary Clinton received around 2.8 million more popular votes than Donald Trump, but Trump won the electoral college vote 304 to 227.

Although Donald Trump didn't win the popular vote in the 2016 presidential election, he still became president because he had more than enough electoral votes. This way of electing the president makes some people feel as if the popular vote doesn't matter.

Direct
ELECTIONS

Although the Electoral College system can be hard to understand, other elections in the United States are easier. In direct elections, people vote for a candidate, and the candidate who receives the most votes wins and takes office. In these kinds of elections, every vote matters.

Even in the case of the Electoral College, an individual's vote can still make a difference. The winner of the popular vote in a state is generally given all the state's electors. Because of this, the popular vote still means something in a presidential election.

Know the Facts!

Members of the U.S. Senate were chosen by state legislatures, or lawmaking bodies, until 1913. That year, the Constitution was amended, or changed, to allow for the direct election of senators.

Direct elections are held on local, state, and national levels.

A DIFFERENCE

Americans sometimes feel as if one vote won't make much of a difference in a big election. This is mostly true in elections held in states and cities with large populations, where it would be very unlikely for an election to come down to one vote.

People often feel this way when their **political** views are different from those around them. If a state or community generally elects members of only one political party, someone from another party may not vote because they believe the candidate they would vote for won't win.

Know the Facts!

In a presidential election, states in which both the Democratic Party and Republican Party have nearly equal amounts of support are called swing states.

In a big city, it can be hard for one person to feel as if their vote matters.

Worth
FIGHTING FOR

Although some people believe their vote doesn't matter, certain groups of people fought—and some even died—for the right to vote. When the United States first became a free country, African Americans and women couldn't vote. After many years, the Constitution was amended to grant them this right.

Even after the Constitution was amended, African Americans often had to pay taxes or take tests before they could vote. In 1965, the Voting Rights Act was passed to end these unfair practices. This long struggle for equality shows how much the right to vote matters.

Know the Facts!

African American men were granted the right to vote when the 15th Amendment was passed in 1870. Women were granted the right to vote in 1920, with the passage of the 19th Amendment.

People fought for the right to vote throughout U.S. history. It mattered so much to them that they were willing to go to jail and **risk** their lives for it.

A Lack
OF TRUST

In the past, people fought for the right to vote because they believed their vote could make a difference. Today, however, that belief isn't as strong. In the 2016 presidential election, less than 56 percent of Americans who could vote actually voted.

Some people don't believe voting matters because they don't believe in anyone they could vote for. In a 2015 study, only 19 percent of Americans said they trusted the federal, or national, government most of the time. This lack of trust is one reason some people choose not to vote.

Know the Facts!

A 2017 study showed that 25 percent of Americans who didn't vote in the 2016 presidential election chose not to because they didn't like anyone running or the things they stood for.

Some Americans feel the politicians they read about don't really care about them, so they don't think it matters who they vote for—or if they vote at all.

A Right and a
RESPONSIBILITY

People who believe in the importance of voting may not always like how the government is doing things. However, they believe voting is a way to create change. Nothing would ever change if people didn't vote. It's the best way for citizens to make their voices heard.

Voting is a right and a **responsibility**. U.S. citizens are given many freedoms, but they have a job to do, too. Part of that job is voting. A democracy only works if people **participate** in it, and voting is the main way to do this.

Know the Facts!

In a 2015 study, 79 percent of Americans said having democratic elections was very important.

Exercising the right to vote is seen by many as an important part of being a U.S. citizen.

Building a Stronger
DEMOCRACY

Respecting different points of view about voting is important. People who believe voting matters can help people who think it doesn't matter understand the reasons they should vote. People who don't think voting matters can share their point of view to help leaders learn how to make everyone's voice feel heard and valued.

Free and fair elections are often seen as one of the most important parts of a democracy. Understanding all the different points of view people have about voting can help make a democracy stronger.

Know the Facts!

More than half of all Americans believe ordinary citizens can **affect** how the country is run, according to a 2016 study.

Does voting matter?

YES

- Every vote counts in a direct election, which is what most elections are.

- The presidential candidate who wins the popular vote in their state is generally given all the electors in that state.

- Many people fought for the right to vote throughout history.

- Voting is the best way for a citizen's voice to be heard and to create change.

- Voting is a responsibility for citizens in a democracy.

NO

- U.S. presidents are elected by members of the Electoral College and not directly by voters.

- The winner of the popular vote doesn't always become president because of the Electoral College.

- It's very unlikely for a big election to come down to one vote.

- Many people believe politicians don't care about them and their needs.

- Most Americans don't trust the government.

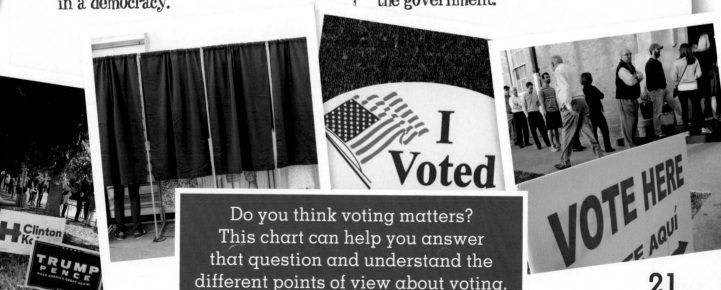

Do you think voting matters? This chart can help you answer that question and understand the different points of view about voting.

GLOSSARY

affect: To produce an effect on something.

candidate: A person who runs in an election.

debate: An argument or discussion about an issue, generally between two sides.

participate: To take part in.

political: Relating to government and beliefs about how governments should work.

popular vote: The choice shown through votes cast by the general voting public and not representatives.

process: A chain of actions needed to make something work.

responsibility: A duty that a person should do.

risk: To put in danger.

For More
INFORMATION

WEBSITES

Election Central: Election Process

pbseduelectioncentral.com/election-process.html

This website features helpful videos explaining different parts of U.S. elections.

U.S. Electoral College

www.archives.gov/federal-register/electoral-college/about.html

The U.S. National Archives and Records Administration created this website to explain the Electoral College process.

BOOKS

Almasy, Kip. *Why Voting Matters*. New York, NY: PowerKids Press, 2018.

Conley, Kate A. *Voting and Elections*. Minneapolis, MN: Core Library, 2017.

Ford, Jeanne Marie. *How Elections Work*. Mankato, MN: The Child's World, 2017.

INDEX